DREAMS AND DREAMERS

A BOOK OF POETRY
BY
LYNN COHEN

BLUE LIGHT PRESS ❖ 1ST WORLD PUBLISHING

1ˢᵗ WORLD
PUBLISHING

SAN FRANCISCO ❖ FAIRFIELD ❖ DELHI

Dreams and Dreamers

Copyright ©2010 by Lynn Cohen

1ST WORLD LIBRARY
106 South Court Street
Fairfield, Iowa 52556
www.1stworldpublishing.com

BLUE LIGHT PRESS
1563 45th Avenue
San Francisco, California, 94122

BOOK AND COVER ART / DESIGN
Melanie Gendron
www.melaniegendron.com

FIRST EDITION

LCCN: 2010943504

ISBN: 9781421891958

DREAMS AND DREAMERS

ACKNOWLEDGMENTS

I would like to acknowledge the following media where some of these poems have previously appeared: in *Quickenings; Freshet; Mobius; Long Island Quarterly;* the *Literary Review; Long Island Sounds; The Long-Islander; Creations; The Poet's Art; Poetz; Poetica; Soul Fountain; The Pedestal Magazine;* on *Poetryvlog;* and in my chapbook, *Lonestar Days.*

Dreams and Dreamers is dedicated to my daughter, Natasha Carrie Cohen. May you continue to dream . . .

Thanks to long-time friend, inspiration, very talented writer and Blue Light Press Chief Editor Diane Frank. Also to Stephen Dunn and posthumously to W. D. Snodgrass for their inspiration. Finally, I would like to thank the Long Island Poetry Community —most notably, Tammy Nuzzo-Morgan, Cliff Bleidner, George Wallace, David Axelrod and Gayl Teller—for all its efforts in promoting this art here.

CONTENTS

Dreams and Dreamers

Mentors and Lovers

Places—Real and Imaginary

Metaphorical Times

Dreams and Dreamers

DREAM CATCHER

I dreamed about you
Again
I guess it was the future
Can dreams be set then?
I know fantasies can . . .
in the longed for when.

You wore a pony
gray and pulled back.
Tall and a bit frail
almost a composite
you climbed a long-ago ladder
as other people passed—
from my past.

The sky outside
was duller than your hair;
overcast like your mood,
and I knew
it was a nightmare.

SLEEP LAND

In Davy Crockett pajamas
coonskin cap slanted sideways
holster, shells and belt
your bunk bed above a younger brother
lying on old west threads
forbidden comics hidden for another night
tossing to the drone of a distant television
sleep was easy:
no nightmare scares
scars years away—
while summer burns remain forever;
Reese Beach tattooed permanently
in memory.

DREAMS AND DREAMERS

Summer's end again:
an almond tree,
sweet, hard nuts,
the tart taste of tongue-laced kisses—
soft like a southwestern rain shower.

My hair traces our lips
tangles with your mustache
your fingers caress
my breasts
tan; tentative
after too many years
too many changes
too many mixed messages.

Tall; taut; tired;
gaunt; grayer; with
teeth stained by coffee and cigarettes;
your face inflamed in a perpetual flame.
Time has not been kind
to dreams and dreamers.

"A Dream Within a Dream" (Edgar Allan Poe)

Days segue
only one way
              back
to an afternoon last June
"A dream within a dream."
Your eyes the color of my poems—
Desdemona green
hair albino straight:
like frost
draped in stars
in stripes
in blood
in lives lost.
Marchers
moving through Manassas;
Manhasset;
Baghdad
carrying coffins of children,
who skated on Caroons Lake
drank whipped chocolate
went to Kindergarten
a whisper ago—
babies bathed in primal guilt
boys in Christian Academy blazers
bowing to the brothers
halls I crisscrossed
before the towers
before I had Kabul with cream cheese
and a bagel—
every morning memory in the making.

LATE FOR THE SLEEP LAND EXPRESS

Late for the Sleep Land Express;
the last skater has left the ice, and
after a perfect program
awaits her prize.

She is far from hometown Tokyo—
with its sun-embedded flag;
away from deepening night;
time confused
like Billy Pilgrim, she has seen her future.

I am in my heated bed
having taken the Express before
serenity assuring a long rest
my future is assured.

I saw it on Sunday
among unnatural lighting
and windowless chambers,
people in open tombs,
lying in every room,
my entire past greeting me,
and my mausoleum awaiting.

Dreaming Is for Free

You tell me,
"It was meant to be"
dreams that lead to reality
jungles of Jungian trees
I climb in my poems
plaited corn rows
soft as the summer
running up his hands
and down yours
in time's eye,
where childhood hides
behind places you can no longer find—
bars and candy stores and
the girl in the next-door neighborhood.

Memories we share of times we did not share
in Washington Square; on Waverly Place
when I ran mad
and miserable.

EXILES

The arboretum cuttings
of many autumns
have come and gone
along with all the exiles.
While we were caught in a French café
playing our own end game,
the pawns wept for Margaret
and I for you.
I became so tired of playing checkmate
with my own life.

So my mind wandered
to a peach-scented summer,
when trees shaded a redwood deck
dropping their fertile gifts
at my feet.

Fecund and full
I awaited your birth:
My first;
My only;
I remember this clearly,
though thirty years have passed,
and the black clone dogs
left long ago,
I still dream them
in my mother's garden,
plundering cherry tomatoes
under sky-white whispers
when time held promises
it never delivered.

BURNING BRIDGES

A mango moon ribbons spring
sprinkles orange light on Washington Square,
where we walked
past hanging paintings,
when everyone was young.

Then, one-by-one, they were gone,
even the dog,
whose china clone claws at my memory;
gnaws away the days.

Even so, I thought
I would know
when you returned—
silver strands of tousled hair;
hazel eyes;
younger than I.

Pulling me to fantasy;
sharing memories of times we did not share:
Sheridan Square;
MacDougal Street;
the Louvre
the Tate
the Trevi Fountain and the Spanish Steps
ancient artifacts under
the Bridge of Sighs and all
those bridges burning in the distance.

BROKEN BOY

"Write about what haunts you."
—*Frank Bidart*

Your lips taste of fall:
warm cinnamon apples and cider;
when petals are lost; sheep gone,
and I long for forbidden sport.

Your hazel beads gaze;
we are alone in time and space.
Life erases itself,
and as I reach for taut, tapered fingers;
hands that held mine; held me minutes ago,
I do not know how we began
or if we will end
or even if we were.

In wet July berries, we were not real.
Then, our lips kissed, and
nights did not end;
days stretched into the next
back to Washington Square,
when my grandmother was my age,
and I walked through the arch;
played in the park
in those post-polio summers.

Now that I am nearly over,
I dream of dead dogs clothed in plaid;
you wrapped in a blue sweater
sitting rows in my past
a broken boy in a broken world
wandering a haunted, wasted land
fodder for today's nightmares
that steals my sleep.

MID-LIFE BOYHOOD

A blue moon on a New Year's night
so late in life
silhouettes geese swarming
against a stark sky
as you appear buoyant
darting like a windhover
apple-cheeked in mid-life boyhood.

Another child of a boy
pulled his lips from me and
went to where clouds never lingered longer
than a single rainbow,
and when he returned,
I was gone:
to kinder; to grad school; to hearth and wifedom.

Yet he lives in my memory of
a distant Christmas celebrated
in a church in Montmartre—
snow splattering stained glass
fronting the fireplace of our souls
as we stared into the street-lamp muse below
while the Priest said mass, and
thirty years passed.

STOLEN IMAGES

Pajamaed and pampered
pram pusher in tow
Plandome long past,
he called you "Da-Da"
decades ago
grams of notes
floated
ice-smoked snow
slid hours away,
and he was grown
leaving empty places
we have all known
now the Southern Cross anticipates:
wet, humid mornings
summer's beloved moorings
mallards' green-peak plumage
preening in my last season
and fading like molting feathers
at fall break

EMILIE GLEN'S LOFT

Boys in too tight jeans
hair hugging their torsos
flowing over flawless skin
in apartments above MacDougal
hardwood floors hard on our backs
summer incense sweet
scents mingling with the streets' below
so many years ago
I walked to a fruitier
across Broadway,
where ancient men played chess
day after day
huddled winters near fires they made.
Fingers in cut-out gloves
frozen in memory.
In fall, Little Italy awoke to
tables laden with canapés.
January welcomed the Chinese New Year
with red and gold fireworks' fragments
sake and plum wine.
April brought cherry blossoms;
impressionist brush strokes;
soft buds blooming briefly.
Another summer found you in a loft
the music of poetry your muse
refusing to share the night.

THE YEARS

This time
the sacrifice is mine
as early June berries
bring back ripe summer mornings
when we walked on wide clay beaches.
I three and topless
your pineapple shirt open
 revealing hair everywhere.

I could not foresee
that back-to-back day
decades later
when my child frolicked with her father
in a blue, blow-up pool
two and nearly naked
splashing unabashedly.

Now I read Bergson and Proust
lament my fears
watch ancient women don masks of yesteryear.

MATISSE MOMENTS

The half-light
of late fall
finds us
forgotten
under quiet covers

The squall of gulls
entertains us
as you gulp
early morning coffee
puff that first cigarette
blow indoor snow away
in a late night hotel
known for sparseness
and little else

Reflected in ceiling mirrors
hours dance away
a Matisse painting
pink and blue
and bold
holds us for only this moment

CONFESSION

I passed St. Aidan's
where you kneel and pray
blessed by St. Margaret Mary Alacoque
holy days of obligation; every Sunday
and remembered:
illicit touches
endless hugs we denied existed
kisses soft on softer lips
naughty missives.

We were teasing teens—
though we are not 16 . . .
players in an endless end game;
we did not say what we meant
nor mean what we said;
we had a near affair and missed it.

You have been this path before—
running partners
train companions
vixens with vibrant locks
compose your history
of daily dalliances
despite your perfect life
and literary wife.

MENTORS AND LOVERS

Winter Solstice

For Stephen Dunn

Students line oblong sides
of a plush parlor
plump chairs
front a fireplace.
The years die away
as my poet
quotes Baudelaire
chops metaphors
stomps muses
undoes images
defines tone
entwines voices
reads about love:
wives and ex-wives—
the places we have all been.

His beret covers
what the decades cannot
but I can see
what I have always seen:
neat hair and beard
I can hear
an erudite speech
that has always been there
as I close my pupils
sit among my school children
feel my mortality and grieve.

ON THE DEATH OF W. D. SNODGRASS

You loved blondes with blue eyes
replaced them when they turned wives
forty-five to my 19
I was Larissa
in that near Russian winter
defying your misogyny
I navigated ice tunnels and became my future:
Moved away and continued to write
questing for an inspirational chalice
addicted muse
holier than thou grail
and found you on every rail
on the trail of summer;
the tail end of late autumn
in each turning of the equinox
in Indiana late one February
on Long Island in his alcohol-laced lips
in His November kisses
cold by sleet time.
But now that you are gone
I will know when you try to reappear in another form.
I will sacrifice the poems
for sleep
And self-induced suffering is no longer a treat—
for I am older than you when we met.
Yet very much saddened by your death.

Runaway Rabbit

(In memory of John Updike)

Rain falls in icicles:
too cold to melt Connecticut's brittle snow:
where black ice graves blanket the roads;
the A & P has changed names, and
rabbits sleep till spring.

You are in a perpetual sleep:
poker games and icy lanes
gone with key exchanges
and yesterday's wives
now engaged in their own lives.

You filled my wait
thirty winters ago
amid the Ayatollahs
veiled Iranian women
and stoning
as I read *Rabbit Redux*
and *The Witches of Eastwick*
eyed my husband suspiciously
whenever we quarreled
thought life would change
but now that she is thirty
I am scared
that this is all there is.

FRAGMENTS

Camellias bloomed late that summer
Sweetly perfumed
Among the vaulted ceilings
And mosaics
The spanking pure pews
And white dress
All those beginnings that have ended

The memories you share
Exeter and Manlius
Smith and Colgate
All sound like a college catalog

The ones you do not
Unlock
The bear skin rugs
And winter fires

The gamekeeper
You wrestle
Fathers and sons
Sons and lovers
And the gentleness within

Tenderness frames you
A tendril of unruly hair
falls forward
You brush it back
And it returns
Again and again
In the fragmented moments
Of the trusted present
In the quiet drone
Of the eastern ocean
On an autumn afternoon

SOLSTICE KISSES

Promise me
Nights that last to noon
Lean limbs
Green eyes
Tiny scars
A sidebar
Mustache
Carefully groomed
Hair the color of summer suede
Share my life
My strife
My writings
Spontaneous solstice kisses
Impulsive and perfect
Against February tides
Tidings that dreams are made of
Walks on winter beaches
Strokes from my fingers to your
Strong hand
Almost incestuous
For you are
The forefather
I forever the child
In the snowdrift moments

MY MOTHER'S LOVER

Blush blue and charcoal skies
another wintering
your lips dry and sweetly red
brushed my forehead
my mother's lover

The fireplace segued
purple-flamed rhythms
gentle curls and
quiet, hazel eyes
burn in every memory
my mother's lover

You missed decades
by dying that spring
while the earth was hard
your grandchildren unformed
our dogs not yet born
now with you, too
my mother's lover

E-Z RIDER

He roared away
New York City smoke everywhere
Hair the color of carrots and the cat
the autumn air a pollutant

No Rhodes scholar
An Ivy keg
And camp sweatshirt
Piece together his past

Fraternity connections
Love of economics
Receding hairline
And a 401K his present

Yet I dream of carrot-topped grandchildren
"Hurry up; it's time."
I am running out of time
To run after toddlers
Hands smeared in another generation
I don't even know where the last one went

Yesterday she cried in pink, newborn rage
Played for days after days
Left for kindergarten and college on the same day
As I ignored my thirties
My forties
My fifties
Loved a child of a man:
martini slurping
excitement-churning
intense soul.
Three years without rest
I continent hopped in carceral spaces.
White noise
and goats my solace
found out time could not be stopped
in autonomous moments,
yet the memories persist
long after I thought they could
long after I knew they should.

GRANDFATHER

Every winter Sunday
my grandfather drove to the country
to visit his mother's grave.
He left M & Ms
on the windshield of father's car—
passing Massapequa back to Jersey.

My grandmother road along,
and when he was gone,
she still signed my cards
the two of them.

Now the quiet tick/tock of your Grandfather Clock is
nestled near a Netflick
its pendulum a somber drum
tapping away our evenings.

ELAINE

Misty, moonless moments
Manhattan
The last of August
Two blocks past therapy
And decades ago

You cling to her memory
Despite your clones
Provincial and boring
clawing

Long for the manic mementoes
Of mornings that lasted forever:
inside out shirts
damp with the day's love
soaped and fresh skin
new and young
reborn

MARCIE

The Ohio of your youth
brushes the soft, sepia memories—
book stalls, ancient stores
along the muddy waters.
Juxtapose her bright purple
and
fuchsia Sunday dress
with forbidden fruit,
your Adam's apple.
She slithered toward your raw haunches
eyes, bare slits
snake-like and merciless.
You writhed in her snare
unconscious, bare, daring.
"Carpe diem,"
you screamed
twenty-five winters ago.

MARTA

Just past Haight Ashbury
and the summer of love
auburn hair aglow
against late autumn's palette
and southern California's forever young
ravishing and refreshing
Marta was no smarter than the rest
another in your midlife crisis
that lasted a lifetime
a month of lust
passed into decades of dreams
now seventy
her great-grandchildren gather
around as for an Uncle Remus tale
she sits enveloped in gray braids
and love beads
her brocaded skirts swish
to the rhythm of her cane
yet on still nights
a conch shell carries the sounds of the years back.

PLACES—REAL AND IMAGINARY

IRISH SUMMER

Clotted cream
warm scones
shorn sheep painted blue
grazing in emerald pastures.

Where you linger in every memory
in the echoes of Lady Gregory
in Joyce and Nora
and Maude Gonne
among the many tenors
on the road toward Cork and Galway.

I fled to forget
yet your smile blooms in mine,
and your touch is reflected
in the yellow rose-garden
back-lighted by the midnight sun.

There is too much death back home
this wet season
more wakes await my return.

IRELAND 2009

Women wrapped in scarves
walk to mass
like 40 years never passed
tight couples move on cue
circle glasses of Guinness,
and I think of your kisses
startling compliments
Is it Ireland:
the late evening sunlight
quiet sheep
and sleeping cows
men driving horse buggies?
Where I can barely find a computer
nobody has a Blackberry,
and my cell searches for no service
my room has no clock
even CNN is timeless
I am permanently jet lagged,
yet my complaints are ignored;
maybe I need to be laid back
throw out my five-year plan
hope my CV gets hit by lightning
move to Brigadoon—
But I would miss the kitten.

The Bus Went to Portlaoise

The bus went to Portlaoise
past ancient trees and endless pubs
people in Celtic costume.

I wanted a tour guide,
but got a disgruntled driver
riding the wrong side of the road.
So I pulled my seatbelt tighter;
tried to remember the "Hail Mary."

As a Jew, I had avoided mass at Maynooth.
While a Jesuit gave communion,
dispensed wine and wafer,
I went to the Internet Café,
bookstore, bank and bakery
pretended to be in Paris
among glasses of Guinness and dark cider
in an outdoor café
on the Champs Elysées.

LONDON

Yellow pools
of moonlight
Strolls along the Thames
Matisse and Picasso
The Tate
A private tête-à-tête
You and Kate

When you are old
The millennium Ferris wheel
    Will churn
In your mind
And remind you
    Of this time

In Paris

Paris,
a dead cigarette in summer
at the Sorbonne,
the ghost pale faces of the bouquinistes on the Rive Gauche,
clouds that skim the roof swiftly
and pass to death,
where New York scars
cannot heal.
For even in Paris
as a pigeon
comes home to me
bringing back
inseparable memories
in my flight
I find
there is no
away from loneliness;
clouds only circle
the same path . . .

PARIS

Share with me
my memories of Paris:
a mélange of impressions
indelible painted images
inked in my soul.
I am my own Japanese pillow book.
I wear my words on my skin.
Fragmented mots of tarnished moments
tied together by silver threads
and misted over like the earth
on an early day outing
along the Bois de Boulogne.
Skin taut and pink as the beads
on the necklace you gave me
a Matisse deep pink
on a soon-to-be-distant birthday
so late in life.
I was surprised
I can still feel the dampness
of late spring's longing.

LAST TANGO REDUX

You promised me Paris
one more time.
We would walk the Tuileries
full with rose blossom spring.
Wander the Louvre,
lost in Renoir's and our own autumn dances.
Sip cappuccino in Montmartre;
eat a Madeleine in Montparnasse.
Your arm brushing my back
possessive; playful.
We pretend there are no expectations,
but there always are.

So dance the last tango with me
rapidly,
Olé! Olé!
Get those feet in step:
one, two, three,
before the entanglement ends.

Pilgrimage Chez Père Lachaise

The places I remember
belong to the Proustian past—
the appearance of Madame Swan on altered streets.

Memories of Fifth Avenue afternoons:
browsing Brentano's
the peal of St. Patrick's bells
the appeal of Picasso's goat
the Lizard King in nearby New Haven.

In Paris, Sartre and Simone having a difficult relationship,
which we shared,
yet you convinced me I was happy,
for seven years.

Not as unhappy as Plath
I managed to survive.
But now I dream of Père Lachaise.
In a time near death.
Will I be buried near Balzac?
Will my tomb make the map?
Become a shrine?
Will April bring pilgrims on their Chaucerian journeys—
praying to the Mother of God
that their sins be erased?

STAINED GLASS PROMISES

The years are mixed together
in stained glass champagne flutes.
They shatter and fragment
like a bombed marble obelisk
in a Paris church
circa 1940.
Held together by golden threads
these goblets
mirror Paris in the millennium
the city of lights
year-long fireworks
churning Ferris wheels
and flashing towers.
I remember the Sorbonne,
the Rive Gauche so long ago.
For where are the bouquinistes?
And the pigeons of a quarter century past?
Lost with my parents
in the holocaust that is time
like the dusty remnants of a photograph album
now silent people staring from its pages.
Yes, perhaps London is better
with its perpetual fog.
Continuity is kinder
than stained glass promises.

BRESLAU

Walk with me
share snow laden lanes
and stark winter crosses
too recent graves
past your own life

The poinsettias are red
as the blood of Christ
he dispensed on Sundays
to people who still remember

You have passed this way before
Dover Street marks a vicarage
fuels flames
from a faraway flight

You were here in some time
your shadow is implanted in the winter cactus
caught by the perpetual pinwheels
that forever point toward your past

In the primal hours
of the private present
in the recent memories
of your taut presence
I seek
a personal communion
in the broken winter land
far from the shared bread and wine

Yom Kippur at Breslau Cemetery

Stones and stars
Auschwitz and Dachau
Fade
Into fall graves
Time's tattoos
Numbers and designs
Straight lines
hide
German soldiers
Or those who could have been

Around the bend
The Jewish section
A fasting Sabbath
Another new year
The Shofar sounds
My agony
Away

SATURDAY NITE LATE IN LIFE

A man who could cook
Did I want him?
No.
Even though I eat cold cereal
Hate to market

A man with his own garden
who grew his own food
worked an organic farm
with legs nicer than mine
offered tomatoes and cukes
as exchange
for shared winters'
warmth
by a wood stove
Did I want this?
No.

A place to meditate
sheep who graze
chickens for fresh eggs
a bed floating on the floor
my own private door.
Did I want this?
No.

It is just too late.
I want to sleep past eight.
eat popcorn for dinner
and maybe a chemical or two.
My electric blanket is quite cozy
big enough for one.
The Dairy Barn has all I need
I don't even have to leave the car.

Another woman
draped in fear
fertile and scared
will share
his life
his strife
become his wife.
inherit my scars.

PEARL SKY DAYS

Almond-scented afternoons
wet, yellow and timeless
fragrant in memory
blend Baltimore
with the way you feel
on a Long Island morning

Early coffee cups
and shells I can't forget
juxtapose
another war
waging against a CNN backdrop

Your lean torso
t-shirted and terse
relaxes to my rub
tension lessens from my touch
on that pearl sky day
I have never forgotten

Scarlet, scattered stones
lost in a month of moments
we pass
monuments from the past
thirty years have passed
yet it's all the same
the same poets read
As I still search for mentors
for immortality
and love

The End of Nothing

That cool spring night
poetry played
music of long ago
You held me forbiddingly
kissed me in the foreshadows
of today's pain

I know I knew you
in the glistening snow
the icy paths
among the Red Raiders
banging basketballs
espousing Kierkegaard and Sartre
"In our Time"
when "Church Going"
became a memory,
and I loved a priest-to-be
and a man who loved other men.
Now
how can something that never was
hurt so much?

The Christening

Splashes of canvas
square and rectangular frames
fill a tiny open space
in a quiet gallery
outside industry awaits a work week
inside the poet
freeze frames the past
amidst the red and blue hues
in this new venue.

Lunch is Zagat rated, he notes.
I note a pink-bundled baby
carried in to the eatery
grey-suited brothers flanking her
smiling young parents
misshapen relatives
in odd, colorful costumes.
I feel my dowdy, professorial self
weekend jeans and turquoise
to set off my eyes
no othotics yet
as those worn by the godmother
brandishing a waist-hugging cross.

And I think of the death of your professor
of long ago
and wish it were my christening
or even my child's.

FOR NATASHA

Further back
in a January day
I have never forgotten
I cried
the tears you cry tonight
damp drops staining the photographs
of their times
like a May mist
that settles in for life.

And as the beating rain
taunts me to wallow
in the memories it evokes
I succumb
and travel far, far back
to a quiet bay
a small beach; a track house
and journey through too many
difficult days.

As the year's passing
is marked
by outgrown clothing
and marred by overgrown tombstones.

SNOW IN APRIL

Snow in April
hides the daffodils
disguises the turf
cloistered inside
I dream of his scent:
eucalyptus trees
English Leather
spring grass

I remember
we loved on musk-damp mornings
cicadas beating the screens
crows competing for symphony seats
scarlet tanagers preening

When I touch your straight
white tufts
and bristle beard
I stare in despair
at your tight cable arms
formal shirt
pressed pants
shined shoes
and know it is not you
I am seeking.

METAPHORICAL TIMES

TRAIN WRECK

A damp August day.
Rain beats my memories away.
I match it tear-for-tear.
Turn toward the stalwart stories stored
star-ward and re-explore.

Every late summer forecast
puts me in pain
from someone I was not supposed to have
while hallucinating trainmen
with white flags
    waving;
                indicating;
                              begging;
                                            calculating;
                                                      expecting
me to hop on board
travel toward a broken rail
escape as my car de-rails
be sidetracked by another.

But I am taking my own car.
driving dark nights;
days in a fugue,
where I can tell this burnt orange autumn
from other mulching times.

Years are linear:
lined up for the plucking
the cluck of a million chicks to the slaughter
the murder of pet pigs for food.
a daughter to wife to mother;
a season when I will no longer be here.

Box Cars

Pain again
as a distant train horn
warns of a pending storm.
Descending downward,
my moods are altered
this cold midnight
when sleet coats my car:
winter's wax,
and I am scared
of your clean-shaven beard,
the sensual curves of your poems,
the piece of soul you may take.

For I am old.
My friends collect diseases like chess pieces.
I get my medical know how from info-mercials.
The shows that appeal are for seniors—
no MTV, for me:
teens gyrating
their counterparts springing from rooftops;
extreme sports—
just the bike to nowhere is extreme these days.

Yet your words parch my lips;
your strophes spark desire,
parse arguments, and I am defenseless in my descent.

ALL OUR ENDS

In my naissance
the brown and beige oval-faced hours
of effacement
are all our ends.

There at the cusp of the Tigris and Euphrates Rivers—
may be my memories of
baptism by green and blue swirling drops;
being dunked in time's currents.

For I am all my sisters:
veiled and unveiled
eastern and western.

I read Proust in Persia
Nabokov in Iraq
follow Indira to Iran
and back again;
pray for peace every day
bowing to the east—Mecca
and Medina.
The Western Wall
The Great Wall of China, too,
are my refuge.

OCTOBER BIRTHDAY

In the clear, crisp mornings
The dew-covered moments
Of apples and honey
pumpkins and cider
Fall dons a costume
fantasies and phantoms
Ghastly reminders of our aging
Winter's wrinkles wait
in the starched apartments
the distant hallways
of our future

While candles mark
Another equinox
ninety-six to be exact
refreshments are diet supplements
the guests long dead

Somewhere in London
A daughter walks oblivious
In her own dotage
Closer in Indiana
A boy mourns
What has been lost
In the primal moments
the last Indian summer days

WATERMELON MEMORIES

The street is not altered
all will appear:
gold-laced summer skies
chalked sidewalks
ladies in cashmere and mohair.

Watermelon memories:
wet, pink sweet
seeds spit out
8-millimeter picture shows
tinkling ice cream trucks.

It is just past *Dark Shadows*
watched devotedly by Hattie Ivory.
I was not allowed to see
those long-toothed vampires
and blood roses
my child's future.

Yesterday, I saw a Corvair,
my first car,
an antique,
"vintage," at least,
and I remembered
when I wore a short, white skirt
that hot evening,
and you wet my red forehead
brushed my cheeks
with the beard you had yet to grow.
Now, you push back the hair
that used to be there.

ALABASTER MEMORIES

In the smoked-purple foliage
Of another autumn
Shortening afternoons
And alabaster memories
Skies stained by berries

As the waves overlap into fall
Images dance
Through the squall of seagulls
Carnivores of time's litter
The eroded end of summer

YOU EXIST ONLY IN MEMORY

My memory hears
a mesmerizing Italian melody:
"Al Di Lá; Al Di Lá; Al Di Lá"
strains played at a Seville bull fight
against a Franco red sky
Guernica still at MOMA
Picasso's painting doing time:
animals out of line
characters screeching off the canvas
and causing grim thoughts
to invade my trip
through the Basque Country
toward Tuscany
summer 1970
the Bolshoi dancing in Madrid
mandolins and balalaikas
babushkas and blankets
dotting the backdrop of gypsy camps
twentieth-century pointillism
seen through time's prism
when I wander
in search of lost days
that were stolen away.

APRIL MEMORIES

Pinwheels in Paris
spinning the years
stained-glass past
and paper doll cutouts
Belgian waffles
The purple sky at Shea
imprison
the present
as rain
time's pendulum
beats rhythmically
against night headlights
freeze frames
images I dare not revisit
here again anyway
peasant blouses sheer
dragging jeans
boots through yellow ice flows
your face in the flames
reflections of days so far away
I used to outrun them

Easter 2006

Your words float
in the autumn air
hang on summer rain
cuddle in corners
curl along the deck
cover the pool:
memory and desire.
I long to awaken
in Dublin
with you
anew
near the green-palette mountains
rising from the Irish Sea
at Trinity
or Bray
Let me be Nora
and Frieda
and Maude
And watch the swans swim
and the geese migrate
at Coole
then tightly wrap a sweater
around my future.

EASTER

Our eyes shatter
shards of blue and green glass
prism-like pieces of time
twist in the kaleidoscope
of broken memories
preserved in a camera obscura

I am your Beatrice
All your women the same
Like my men
They interchange
Into archetypal candidates
For a taken job

And you know
As the warm winds blow
Through the church on an April's afternoon
The seasons of planting and reaping and birthing
Are repeating
Over and over
The bodies we have planted
For you are the seed
And I the earth
The primal mystery
Is born another season
In the Easter calling
The tolling bell
And purgatorial fires
the lily moments
a lone figure
rises and offers redemption

PATTERNS I

Massapequa again
as the past and present blend
our memories
of water-green endless days
of time in that same place.

I think I remember
the pane glass view
from my first house
that 1956 world
colors mixed
in a palette of pumpkin and cider.

I think I remember
years after years
the purple-flamed rhythms
of all those fires
of all those beginnings that have ended.

To be back here
with you
is to repeat and begin anew
the cycle I forever ride
through the patterns of my life.

PATTERNS II

A carousel horse stops for me,
and I get on.
He promises to take me forward,
but I know
this ride only goes around
and around.
So like my continuing life
lived between the cracked sidewalks
of my imagination,
I wander the alleyways of this
time and another,
and journey back to my grandmother's apartment
in Greenwich Village.
I see it always
in its pre-War splendor
with two bathrooms
and a fireplace—
looking down on MacDougal.
And I see her dignified in
her bun and bedroom slippers
for that last trip
to the Eighth St. Waffle House of death

Patterns III

The elusive strains
of my father's mornings
haunt me
as early day noises
from my own life
quiet and distant
run through my thoughts.

I remember him lathered in soap
as I pretended to shave, too
in my Dr. Denton world, where
like the pieces of a broken mirror
nothing ever fit afterward.

I remember the comings and leavings
the dark night airports
and smoke-lit train stations
all purple in the hazy tunnels of today.

I remember waving and crying
the final early goodbye
the nails, the lowering, the tears.

I have relived the patterns of these mornings
almost never
shoving them into the recesses of streams
of South Pacific waters
pretending the Christmas morning hours
of Chatty Cathy and now old-fashioned skis
are pictures of someone else's life
tucked in the basement album of a far-away family.

I walked these years
away from you
away from the hurt and loneliness
of a thousand empty Sunday afternoons
while you flew away your days
on blonds, on brunettes, on alcohol
on denying time
as it passed through anyway
like a hungry passenger through a closed dining car.

Patterns IV

The anguish of August city afternoons
wandering through Matisse and
steamy, deserted streets
dreaming of what could have been:
the beat of steady water on country roses;
love mine to choose.

My life is like a French film
with a choice of endings;
a subway car with too many stops.
I forever ride nowhere
in an aisle-less, window-free world,
where signalmen have taken over the route,
and I cannot choose the pattern
any more than dinner guests choose the china.

But I can select the sheets
matching and pressed
for a bed ready to take on new lovers—
honeysuckle yellow
in their almond sweetness;
these sheets taunt me
to rise with
the short-lived laughter
of my children in the yard, and
toss out 15 years
to an overpaid carting company
to soar with the patterns and
fly with the rhythms
of other days.

VIRGIN IN AMERICA

(for Kevin Johnson)

To wake up a virgin in America
on a water-green day
when clouds are distant and far apart
and the air blows through you
like the wind through an un-reaped field.

ABOUT THE AUTHOR

Lynn Cohen was nominated for the 2006 and 2010 Pushcart Prize for Poetry. She gave a scholarly paper at the Gerard Manley Hopkins Literary Festival in 2009 in Ireland. As a result of a grant proposal she wrote, the New York State Council for the Humanities awarded the North Sea Poetry Scene a mini-grant for its "Let's Talk Poetry 2008" series. She has spoken on the works of T. S. Eliot at a National MLA Conference and at local conferences on Christianity and Literature. She also has lectured on modern and post-modern literature, and she has given poetry readings in the United States and in Ireland.

She was a student and mentee of Pulitzer Prize Winners Stephen Dunn and W. D. Snodgrass. She co-edited The North Sea Poetry Scene's *LI Sounds 2007 Poetry Anthology* and other poetry anthologies.

Lynn teaches at Hofstra University and Suffolk Community College.

Printed in the United States of America